The Resignation

The Resignation

poems

Lonely Christopher

ROOF BOOKS
NEW YORK

ISBN: 978-1-931824-77-4
Library of Congress Control Number: 2018950745

A Note on the Content
Please be advised that this book contains violent themes and language
and addresses sexual abuse, misogyny, homophobia, and other forms of
damage and oppression.

Cover illustration by Wadih Sader
Cover design by Rijard Bergeron

Author photo by Jacob Steinberg

NEW YORK STATE OF OPPORTUNITY | Council on the Arts   This book is made possible, in part, by the New York
State Council on the Arts with the support of
Governor Andrew Cuomo and the New York State Legislature.

Roof Books
are published by
Segue Foundation
300 Bowery, New York, NY 10012
seguefoundation.com

Roof Books
are distributed by
Small Press Distribution
1341 Seventh Street
Berkeley, CA. 94710-1403
800-869-7553 or spdbooks.org

THE ORDER

San Francisco

I used to think that I could draw
and drove a car across the eclipsed
face of the thespian deserts
in a star system so far away from home
that our burning manticores fled
from the harm of a thousand space rats
and worlds died and suns were born
in a way that destroyed human concepts
of time, in a way that recalled the portal
that I once sucked ooze through
when I was first learning how to travel
and fuck for my life.

Magic Bridge

Our glowing failure is always a bridge
the shape of you smoking a cigarette
or skies of me talking to some lady
whose history resembles drowned rainbows
the color that afternoon architects
from firmament to the unruly floor.
We join all consequence with future floor
our pronouns sexy like a flirting bridge
at the conference of wicked architects
like Faust they match a final cigarette
blowing highways of puffs at the rainbows
that barf a loaf thus bridging warm lady.
We get around just fine on that lady
though majuscule events threaten the floor
which we stand fast upon watching rainbows
each colliding into our magic bridge
as surprised I swallow my cigarette
now farting out a world of architects.
There's no such thing as lucky architects
just anthropomorphic bridge's lady
turning to ask you for a cigarette
and when handed it drops it on the floor
where find my cares as monolithic bridge-
like forms all wrapped in carpety rainbows.
It's claimed the dead that came from said rainbows
around this town are awkward architects

who wept into the earth and built a bridge
on sand and the grace of a kind lady
you tell me this you place me on the floor
I smile and ash-flick my pinched cigarette.
My worst for you smells like a cigarette
we kiss and squish bridges around rainbows
all this becomes a poorly wrought dance floor
for our prom date with whispered architects
dressed in fine lace every inch a lady
whose happy birthday lives inside our bridge.
I snuffed my cigarette on architects
you mistook bad rainbows for the lady
who built this floor between us as a bridge.

Little Girls

Like trees
of skin
under the timetable
mother's home
tenses object
an online
of dark branches
the breeze
finding hospital
understood surface
made of
infrequent plastics
this disaster
socks glorified
then disquiet
presented apology
somewhat like
sexy lake
the light reflects
sort of perspective
likely animals
congregations of
entrance strains
the windowed round
soft corners
standing participle

heavily blue
like those things
birthday chandelier
police came
learner mirrored
across concrete
recreational vehicle
sort of night
opaque storm
gone bashes
substitute teacher
fleshy bro
made weather
puffy ache
the shade crucible
wary complication
beguile durance
like bucks
sore protrusion
verb agreement
in the way
the woods scope
colored asks
a whole world
made of
paragraphs
like little girls.

The House of There Is

In this verse is
unbelieving
meaning of all works
and yet people remained.

Voided understanding
of cultivations
as in the next text
expression following destruction
places always fall.

This manner represented the same
ground
nothing but weight
the reason for it
the edge of the words
insist upon it.

There is nothing but pleasure
no manner
difficulty.

There is power
and vast broken light
kingdom a slender thread
the rocks are thrown down.

Justice under the sentence
unchangeable creatures
the mouth stands ready
there is foundation
in full possession
powerful nature
troubled waves of restraint
no security
by any accident.

The unthought persons
innumerable and inconceivable
unsearchable ways
there is nothing
to make it appear ordinary.

Means were never
made use of
there is this clear
place within care
that shall be effectual
escaped the part that matters.

A shadow doubtless
and another reply
dreams of peace and safety
destruction promises
fire in the heart.

There is pleasure in the body
life would avail
the thin air
that is suspended in it.

Descend into the world
nature and end spew
the storm of the present
more and more
higher and higher
and longer the streams
when once it is let
against floods.

Time is rising
justice bends the arrow
the state before unexperienced light.

Form the house of there is
this world closed into morning
there is no other reason
why fear rebukes warning.

Strength and pity
because it's so hard
being will be full
crushing out blood
to shew to love.

Kings of suffering
mighty people burning off
the carcasses.

Despair wrestling
infinite circumstances
representation is young
there is reason to think
discourse promising wonder
now here in this seat.

Known in the house of there is
hanging over the middle
of loud providence
gathering in all parts
that it will be gone before
it is.

The trees fly out
awake to this
behind the mountain.

Modern Marvels

The winter settled round
the guilty house but we got
to the family restaurant
one russet potato makes
a hundred French fries
we took a weird nap in
our realistic nightgowns
we watched the Christmas
tree signaling us with its
slimy undeveloped hands
when the plane crashed
the government freaked
we said jealous prayers
for help in the new year
and in our fancy dreams
a child crept down
to the fountain
to blog.

Nincompoop Insolence Aria

Who knows woman?
like a blown crest:
her voice multifarious
and thoughts various.

Ever rarified belier,
her popular visage
might shine or weep;
trumpery astride her.

How woman flies!
bending in times
to this and that
at the drop of a hat.

Joy is robbed from he
who might trust this she;
for a girl has better plans
in store for basest man.

A male cannot delight
at his imagined right
if syrups of her whole
are less than potable!

A woman is different
as an unreadable text
and all men were born
to befall her sweet hex!

Fag City

And went to the absent god yesterday
There should be laws against that kind of thing
He couldn't tell for sure if I am "gay"
If life has got us down we try to sing
"The crime was never solved," his parents wept
Sometimes he thought that love did not exist
History's ugly lesson hasn't kept
Electorates from propping up fascists
We built a bad relationship from scratch
He punched the windowpane of my remorse
Ambiguous abilities detach
My father threatened an ugly divorce
My mother caught me looking at websites
We moved into the town of constant night.

Bert & Ernie

get married to each   other   whatever
run lace down   main street
        decorate storefronts   all in slutty leather gear
    disturb children   turn boys gay.
you and your boyfriend must fuck each other's
        skeletons out   getting super nasty
        but you guys are no   Bert & Ernie;
    Bert & Ernie   are like   sick-sick in love
        they have one bed   for cuddling
            and another bed   for hardcore action.
    Bert is the top—no duh, power top;
Ernie rides that cock like a real champ
        drives that throbbing dick all ways
                down main street,
like a brand of car poofs buy, all ways down
        to the fucking church   in an
            assless wedding dress
hand down   a choir boy's pants   other hand's
        fingers tormenting the kid's soft curls   so
fucked up.   no,   you feel 'em up, go ahead:
kidnap your favorite,
        enjoy his screams of pain.
            slaughter his innocence and cum on the gore.
        get married to a boy who can't
grow pubes yet rape him in the kitchen
        with a plush doll   shaped like Bert

—<u>monster</u>.

fuck every kid you see   ruined forever

punish their mouths with your giant boner

any   way you want it

indulge every pleasure   destroy family values

turn me into a *Queer Eye for the*

Straight Guy guy   fist me deep,

clutching a shampoo bottle,

smashing my face into an episode

of *Sesame Street*   skull fuck me with

children's programming.   I want you to kill me

back   when I was just a kid

the age of   that choir boy

I woulda liked   a crowbar up my bum   I woulda liked

to be a child bride   your kiddie-corpse adventure.

Oh well but hey

remember don't be shy:

fag up the place will ya   join the

army and molest   soldiers during   combat

and in the bunks   go homo against

their will   brush men's genitals across your lips by accident

give 'em nightmares   queer everything have it

how you like it best   send Bert a ring of

ketamine snorted off a choir   boy's open asshole,

pink   hairless thing

watch Bert jizz in the baby crack and suck it out again;

think of poor Ernie, waiting

at home,   empty butt,   yearning for Bert,

come home   soon
    to fuck him and to fuck him up
        then he'll bleed the sheets up and   dream the day
    whatever   when
they will be wed.

The Demand for a Sign

They came
and began to argue
with him
asking him
for a sign
and he sighed
deeply and said,
"Why does
this generation
ask for a sign?
I say
no sign
will be given
this generation."
And then
he left—
getting into the boat again,
he went across
to the other side.

Thinking of You

In the morning we read in afternoon
We go to the park in the evening we
Dance then at night we sleep today
In the presence of judgment we visit
The largest building in the world in
Summer we go to the beach right on
Schedule you are my loveliest friend
How are you I saw that you went out
Without your coat laughter is healthy
The girl can't stand for it she moans
We get annoyed at her when she says
She hopes that morality doesn't exist
There is nothing to laugh for she says
Was she looking for something was
She guilty of murder surrounded by
Water lined with trees did you know
Many people would like a happy life
We have enough time to do our work
Most of the time I need the book you
Jump for joy like we like all kinds of
Animals I have an irresistible urge to
Leave with you we are leaving are we
Socialists I have a car you don't drive
It I am talking about the facts you are
Talking to me before we sleep at night
We will stay in if it rains like the devil

Water reminds us of a girl in her dress
In the long grass she needs help in her
Disorder everyone supposedly knows
But might have forgotten ask if I hate
Poverty thousands of people don't read
Books we think we are very smart and
We are you wake up early you think it
Looks like rain I am awake Americans
Are masculine what is practical what
Is in context there is some truth to all
Those stories we hear there is probably
A girl in a dress beyond rescue I think
Skyscrapers are masterpieces we hate
A maddening crowd those people are
Crazy you are barefoot abruptly you
Paused and yawned it was cute I saw
Everything in abundance we received
Sad news the same day that very day
It's beautiful the sky small and pretty
She should have shut the door like a
God-fearing tax paying American it
Was my greatest and deepest desire
That I would be with you sleeping
Nobody would molest our privacy
She is so scary she is out of control
The girl had miserable consequences
I recognize that tomorrow we arrive
Other friends came to see us another

Time show me your other hand when
We find the time remember me always
Each morning every day today I do like
Your idea you have about how various
Problems can be solved with long walks
Of all times many a time we ourselves
Appeared from nowhere in an afternoon
After work when we held hands and we
Promised it would be worth it and that
Requires time and a book so gigantic
I wondered if it would fit in the house
No matter what the question is we love
Such a place such things are never said
Such things are never done the leaves
Have all fallen we were asleep a whole
Day all those are all ours all of them in
This whole world everybody everyone
The little girls were so sad we thought
All the little girls were goners will the
Same thing happen to her in her special
Troubles that make me trouble in turn
What a night we had you do remember
See me before the next time I have my
Car my only car my car my beautiful
Car we shook hands kissed and slept
Very lightly at a rough estimate think
Hard always have something in mind
Here is my book keep it with you for

Good luck this is going to seem a bit
Difficult for you to believe but it was
Beautiful to be impossible that weird
Sentence tells me what happened we
Took our friends by surprise they arc
The best tell me what you did and said
We haven't seen anyone haven't seen
Anything that is something interesting
I see nothing I have seen the worst you
Don't talk to anyone I will say nothing
We know everything we know nothing
We forgot everything we understood it
All we Americans are beautiful any day
Any moment one speaks and the other
Listens they tried on new dresses while
We watched they looked at themselves
In the mirrors they looked at each other
They got facedown we walked behind
The group of neighbors congratulatory
But there she was stuck and unsatisfied
We were very glad to escort each other
Into the place so as to be alone together
I understand what is going on I look at
A dark forest at the edge of the beach
In the middle of which a plane crashed
I heard what you were talking about I
Always guess what you are thinking of
It was appreciated in the morning we

Waited it happened the day when she
Had her accident we got up and found
The car look at this picture you know
About this novel by Flaubert are you
Surprised by the government is there
A way to understand how badly she
Is afraid if I hate being late we can't
Leave because of the snow I heard
That story before it's a very funny
Story she drives extremely fast in
My car without my permission we
Were about to say a word we just
Started to leave now we are really
Doing something see the sky above
Our heads look above remembering
How we came across ways to stand
Against the dark to stand out in the
Dark against the dark against sunset
Look ahead straight ahead we have
Shrubs around our house we walk
Home along the river turn around
I am at home standing close to you
At nightfall at your request because
The girl was hiding behind our tree
Other cars came behind mine all it
Does is rain all we want is justice
And equality all we do is play just
Be ready to ask how much money

She needs it rained more yesterday
I wish I could do more for you we
Stay a while together the sun goes
Down when night came we slept
I killed them all at once I did not
Know their names this morning it
Was raining the cold waves spread
Everywhere you go there seems to
Be a feeling of being in place near
And far I follow the wall is about to
Crumble while I write you read the
Newspaper she will come tomorrow
She will stop we will overcome awful
Luck it rained yesterday my book fell
The light went out at night we slept
I did some work you are warm I am
Not worried about anything not even
The devil himself not with you here
With you I can take my suit out from
My suitcase again look at these books
That I have read you have read them
Also she hurt herself falling we had
Remembered the story girls making
Mistakes that sentence you repeated
To yourself all night long from the
Letter that I had written you when
I was away look at these beautiful
Dresses she wears for us I look at

You I must be boring you talking
About how I would not try to kill
Myself but would learn a different
Language instead with some effort
A little support and a bunch of time
You are always by my side nightly
I dream you have always been here
How long have we been here I ask
Have we been living here for long
We must have been here since you
Waited for me if you will just wait
A few minutes more will you help
Me if you do you shall be rewarded
Thou shalt not kill I had finished all
My work you answer when I say hi
If it rained we would not go out why
Should we keep quiet I want to talk
With you I am having fun I noticed
That you had forgotten your book
The vase broke in my hands confide
In me we'll deal with the important
Problems I am seated the sky grows
Darker and turns serious I lay down
On the grass and watch you watching
Me don't try to swim in the lake this
Early in the month we have to go hide
Behind the house they had noticed our
Absence we go to bed every night and

Sleep she got dressed all by herself her
Brain is telling her to do things making
Her cry and fall down the stairs again
But these things are quickly forgotten
I brush my teeth in the morning after
Breakfast the sky keeps growing dark
I don't care about that I like reading
Flowers are placed in vases it looks
Like it might rain we took a walk in
The park the weather getting chilly
I remember this adventure we took
Refuge under a tree I am delighted
With your success the information
Made sense to me when I got home
If we ever oversleep we feel guilty
The car overturned in a ditch she
Was hurt we regret this action she
Committed suicide we will not let
Them in when we are not together
I miss you terribly and you must
Miss me I'll keep quiet won't say
A word if I am doing it all wrong
Stop me you must have left your
Book at home in the morning we
Must be asleep you don't have to
Open the window you might make
It maybe if it rained we would not
Go out she cut herself we too cut

Ourselves we are watching each
Other you are watching me brush
My teeth these are some important
Differences when my wrecked car
Would not start we ran together and
Took shelter under a tree the world
Population increases very rapidly
I am talking to you now American
houses are built with wood I have
A subscription to some magazines
The ground sank I think it all boils
Down to it just being a question of
Not getting caught it is necessary to
Get closer to have a good view you
Too got bored the birds are flying
Away I thought about it and finally
Made up my mind the sky is clearing
Up I wonder what the reaction will be
We fell asleep immediately I cannot
Help but laugh you fell in love with
Me every spring nature comes to life
An obelisk rises in the middle of the
Square you lie down on the sand you
Got used to this climate very quickly
We like reading she is making fun of
Us but she is just a corpse in the rain
Do you realize what the night brings
I woke up twice in the midst of dreams

You came home last night and we slept
We are early risers you left and came
Back before I knew what to do in the
Afternoon today you are early so we
Head for a walk in the park and see
The pastures now we see the forests
Now green pastures offer us a very
Peaceful sight now that we walk to
The bottom of a tremendous chasm.

The Resignation

I.

In last the days I started to reconcile me for my failings private with my wife, Silda, my children, and my whole family. The remorses that I feel will be always with me. The words cannot describe at which grateful point I am for a love and the compassion they showed. Those to which much is indicated, much is envisaged. I was given much: a love of my family, faith and the confidence of the inhabitants of New York, and the chance to carry out this state. I am deeply sorry that I did not live just with what was envisaged of me. In each New York, and all those which believed for in the what I tried to hold me make excuse sincerely. I look at my time as governor with a direction of what could have been, but I also know that in so much as a remarkable civil servant I, and people with whom I worked, achieved much. There is to make much more, and I cannot allow my failings private to disturb the work of the people. During my public life, I insisted believe correctly, that people, independently of their position or power, take the responsibility for their control. I can and will request any less from me. For this reason, I resign of the office of the governor. At the request of Lt. Gov. Paterson, the resignation will be effective on Monday March 17, a date that he believes will allow an ordered transition. I go in front of par with the belief, like the others said, which like human beings, our greater glory consists of never not falling, but in increase each time we fall. Because I leave the public life, I will make the access what I must do to help and cure myself and my family. Then I will test again, apart from policy, to serve the community property and to move toward the ideals and the solutions which I believe can establish a future that hope and that occasion for us and our children. I hope that all the New York will join my prayers for my friend, David Paterson, like it is embark on its new mission, and I again thank the public for the privilege of the service.

II.

In the latter the days, which I began to reconcile me for my weaknesses which are private with my wife, Silda, my children and my whole family. The remorses, which I believe, always is with me. The words can not on, which describe grateful point I for love and the compassion is, which showed up them. Those, to which much is indicated, much is intended. One gave to me much: a love of my family, the faith and the confidence of the inhabitants of New York and the probability to accomplish this condition. I am deeply sad that I did not live straight also, which was intended of me. In each New York and everything those, which believed for on, form what I tried to hold me apology. I regard my time as a governor with a direction of, which it could have been but I while also that inside as much as remarkable civil servants I and people, with which I worked obtains much. There are to form many more and I know my weaknesses, which do not let the work of the people disturb are private. While my public life persisted I believe correctly, people, independently their position or energy, which responsibility for its control take. I can and any of smaller I will demand. For this reason I withdraw of the office of the governor. On requests of Gov Lt. Paterson, is the resignation on Monday, that 17. March, a date effectively, to which it permits an ordered transition believes. I go before equality with the faith, as said the different, as humans, our larger fame never, do not exist to fall, but at increase, each mark if we to fall. Because I leave the public life, I form the entrance, which I must do, around to help and to couriers themselves and my family. Then I examine again to serve apart from politics, the joint property and move toward the ideals and to the solutions, which I believe, can a future, which hope and, which cause our children for us and manufacture. I hope that thanks whole New York my prayers for my friend, David Paterson, how it is began on its new official travel follows and I again the public for the privilege services.

III.

In end when I begin me, my spouse, Silda, child my me and you are reconciled me for my weakness which is the entire family and private use. As for compunction of conscience, I am, that it believes and always. Word those is not possible at on, there is the sympathy to which that describes the point I which, for loving appreciates shows him. Those where many he are shown are intended many. One gave me many: My series of the resident of New York and probability, love that of reliance and confidence completes this word. As for me deeply sad thing I didn't you have lived, in addition the straight line that was I who am intended. In each New York what where I bet me on judgment entirely that at apology, that for at above formal me maintaining. As for I every of years me it considers as the governor who uses direction, whether the person, and I where government employee I who what kind of should be surprised cooperate receive those many, that and could do a so certain thing many in the while I place, but. The shape it is many that, my range depending, you know the work of the person who my weakness, that is not left in the annoyance which is private use. My public servant life that believes me while insisting, the person, their energies which the independent person place or responsibility for her control supports just. I to be possible, because it is smaller, anyone it requires. Therefore I withdraw the office of the governor. Paterson, there are 17 resignation Monday with requesting Gov lieutenant junior grade. The road where March that is ordered is made possible, it considers that date, effectively. As for me before the equality of the reliance us those time the be in order for the reputation where never we are larger with increase, ever since the person, difference, those to go down, not to be each sign it goes. Because I leave public servant life, I help me and me whom that makes with messenger him himself and the entry item which and my family should and is shape is acquired. Then as for me it is useful for the second time, policy, separated from common property you inspect me, the solution which moving I to of ideal believe, future, thing us and the desire which pulls up our children for producing and you are possible. I

how it is, my friend, officially New York of the whole appreciation to of Paterson for servicing my praying privilege is new traveling desire the fact that it continues and the fact that I starts in the public, for the second time.

IV.

In extremity when I begin, my husband, Silda, the mine of child; and you it are reconciled for my weakness which entire family and I use confidential. How for compunction of conscience, by which it always believes to it are expressed those of not possibly is inside further, this there are no attachment to that this describes to the point so, parse of will estimate it is evaluated monster. Those where very healthily shown one much. I gave much to me: My series of the resident of New York and of the probability, love of which confidence and confidence end this word. For me they are deep sad that I didn't you lived, besides the line of skillful line which was that assumed. In each New York which where they to me in the judgment by all that into excuse, this for surplus in officially I which supports. As for each of years I consider as regulator which uses a feeling, if no one, and where the worker of government of which his that type must be it cooperates is obtained those much, than they could make a thing also determined much into the empty one which colic of the I, but the form is much that, my of you knows the work of persona which my weakness, than it is not left into difficulty which I uses confidential. My life of public civil worker to which it believes to me to insistence, persona, their energy which place or the independent responsibility from persona for its control only support. To be possible, because it is inferior, any one to which it requires. Consequence of it extracts the office of regulator. Paterson has 17 to give upward Monday with a question of the young type of Lieutenant Gov. Road where March which he is required presented to possible, this date is examined, it is effective. For me before the equality of the confidence of that of must never because reputation to us where we not to with an increase, is more late on persona, difference, that to go into the bottom, because they there

37

is no each sign whom it goes. Because I leave the life of public civil worker, I help and the I which makes with the same with messenger the article of charm that and they acquire my family and form. After this, for me is useful to the second time, policy, that put outs itself of property the general you it is checked, permission that object of the furniture of ideal believes, future, thing we and the desire it raises our children in order to produce you possibly. I love it, my friend, officially New York entire estimation of Paterson in the order loans the repair services of my privileges to pray the desire of new displacement the custom-house of what it continues and custom-house which it begins in the public, to the second time.

Those That Belong to the Emperor

Magnetic fields of explanation are
Nervously masturbating in public
And she is weeping loudly in her car
The whole goddamn United States is sick.
Last night the mayor's stepdaughter came home
With bruises and black eyes and wouldn't say
If she deserved it but with sickly moans
She told her stepfather to go away.
If some angel of god appeared right now
I'd beat the hell from him mercilessly
And whisper into his broken skull how
I think things worked out with morality.
My spouse is just a piece of porcelain
This month we want to state our vows again.

Rat in the Snow

Billy the Kid killed me, swept the town
Scored sanguinely a wasteland of money
The lasso looped round my pretty neck
His smile burned into the cornea of gods.

Columbia called out to the sea, her breasts
Pointed toward the vertexes of assimilation
My past crimes triggered a recall election
And her statuary benevolences declared us.

Mickey Mouse shot himself in the face, oops
Pulled me under the table to bloodless sport
Ripped off his own shorts and devoured them
I can't think of a time when we felt so alive!

Abraham Lincoln kissed my brow and bled
From a wound in the back of his head, hissy
Maneuvering from heights of production
Fell off my horse and was left for the snakes.

Tom Sawyer inserted his boner into a hole
In the whitewashed fence and a bird landed on it
He stuck his paintbrush inside my mouth, hush
This was the one to which they tied a dying boy.

Frog and Toad are in love, riding bicycles
Into the lake near where the scorpions nest
I wasn't going to say anything but it reminds
Me that the cherriest gift is a rat in the snow.

Blood World

We try loving into the blood, magnanimous.
There is this world; it's got pain and wonder.
Desire nerves, family of killed in their sleep.
Ever surety ends, but all we're entertaining.
"How do you spell that name again?" he said,
And I surely kissed his mouth for experience.
I am enormous, what I take, drear to calculate.
Life: dexterous in prices, timely done withal.
I picture your existence, poignantly disappear
Into a common frustration and awestruck gall.
(There are days better natures feel that they might
Prevail.) A relationship's obfuscation, objected.
The taste in my mouth like forever; say I say I:
A blood world, thus aggravating failure's gallery.
When, again, I gropingly spell toward your light,
Find I only absences; ever word flows too bright.
Descend into total consequence, arrive implicit.
Pleased to be building a home in the worst of it.

Handsome Boy Full of Arrows

This way is us publishing a teen cathedral
        sponsoring convergence
his hips are doomed against
innovation's preciously earned window
kid's sexy tragedy caught within trembling lips
        our entertainment
the direction to the mouth
tracing jejune satisfaction around the fact
        tomorrow is an emergency
details resembling an obscure pageant
as religious awe plays guiltily
with the dangerousness of negative love
his twitching face
        all promise
whispering across our general heart
a definition strung up in athletic composition
to receive punctuation
in conversation a paragraph infinite
our involution's designer gnosis
        this is how poems happen
consequently criminal veneration feasts
terminal event glows beyond mere passivity
        transfigures into style
all proportion now measured
by the achievement of stolid delicacy
hero boy morphing apparatus becoming

luminous ambiguousness

the way form's a meticulous installation

at our field's extremity

this way his injuries deliver him

unto a trope parked glorious

in the subtext of tender harm

the bottom pocket of our appetite.

For Example

for some people a language reduced to its
essentials is a nomenclature a list
of terms corresponding to
a list of things for
example:

The Gettysburg Address

A, a, a, a, a, a, a, above, add, advanced, ago, all, altogether, and, and, and, and, and, and, any, are, are, are, as, battlefield, be, be, before, birth, brave, brought, but, but, by, can, can, can, can, can, cause, civil, conceived, conceived, consecrate, consecrated, continent, come, created, dead, dead, dead, dedicate, dedicate, dedicated, dedicated, dedicated, dedicated, detract, devotion, devotion, did, died, do, earth, endure, engaged, equal, far, far, fathers, field, final, fitting, for, for, for, for, for, forget, forth, fought, four, freedom, from, from, full, gave, gave, god, government, great, great, great, ground, hallow, have, have, have, have, have, here, here, here, here, here, here, here, here, highly, honored, in, in, in, in, increased, is, is, is, it, it, it, it, it, larger, last, long, liberty, little, live, lives, living, living, long, measure, men, met, might, nation, nation, nation, nation, nation, never, new, new, nobly, nor, not, not, not, not, not, note, now, of, of, of, of, of, on, on, or, or, our, our, people, people, people, perish, place, poor, portion, power, proper, proposition, rather, rather, remaining, remember, resolve, resting, say, sense, shall, shall, shall, should, score, seven, so, so, so, struggled, take, task, testing, that, that, that, that, that, that, that, that, that, that, that, that, that, the, the, the, the, the, the, the, the, the, the, the, their, these, these, they, they, they, this, this, this, this, those, thus, to, to, to, to, to, to, to, to, under, unfinished, us, us, us, vain, war, war, we, we, we, we, we, we, we, we, we, we, what, what, whether, which, which, who, who, who, will, work, world, years.

More Right Now a Piano

is recording of mess lividly human
wrought out from a shiny whatever
sorely more right now a piano
than anything scarred disappearing in
celebrity ultra fabric so starched so far away from okay
the ceiling will yawn away around sculptural frames
dreaming into oceanic wallpaper
the machine under wigs yes shapes
like injured religion fits comfortably
in an antique vase of furbished desolation
near enough to canvas as an ambassador of
white becoming blue-pinkish becoming
irritated galaxies of ageless shame
subject simple in shuttering forgiven lids
almost serene agony in disclosure
parts married thinly in automobile parades
across the forehead of recent memory
turning silver before dissolved camera
become here as settee washes out
value the heft of resourceful birthdays
as such but as just as where the heart's
new container factory produced in a variety of colors
but for deliciousness of honest embarrassed lumping
more right now room's true furniture
chewed away with such solvency
all precious news taken fading

within stewed wounds open like cereal

facts accepted menu calmest of snow-pale morning

coloring post-Coca-Cola American advertising

unpacking some morsel-tender humility for

this museum piece of sitting like really bruised fruit

as admission of love

contrastively denial floats

artful programs of similarly combed like-love

spaces universe a weak florescence up against

more right now a piano or

humorless contracts of mushy abuse

caked over before mirroring for those

even private catastrophes may end

worlds defeat of endless whorls emitted

from inside some friendly organ glow

giving out that

it's okay

it's okay

I am.

Sun Came

If the sun came, discoloring the small place, parts
Of the problem would go into storage, you'd toss
Pages of the embarrassing manuscript into the fire,
And this ghost would say, "I love you yet and I am

Burning." This is a world of confusion of worth:
Sullen boys are scoping out the land for a generous
Awning to shelter the precious articles, pellucid skies
For serious poems, great monuments to love scoured

To ranges of salt and bone. Please wire me money via
Western Union: I want to see a flick where a detective
Arrests some fag, marries him in the holding cell, slices
His neck open, does some funny things inside his neck,

And sends the body home. It's possible to shrink into
Nescience, keep the rupture on the Internet, rue
Complicity, and scar the founding of a nacreous
Play that collapses into soft-core, occluded rage

Before the stand. There is no sun in this nation state,
No brightness upon the face; windows, windows! how
Gauche! Why splendor, sky, or fastidious birds—who's
afraid of "What if the sun came?" If the sun came, the sun

Would go away; and this is an unpopular century. "We
Disapprove of the posited scenario wherein in a world
Where the sun came, there would be frequent periods
During which the sky would provide us with a light."

Domestic Relations

the relation between the sex drive and creativity
the relation between the home and its inhabitants
the relation between the architect and his client
the relation between the exterior and the interior
recognizing a socially pervasive perverse dynamic
the woman working into the night in erotic solitude
and her relation to the great American housewife
(chore-free, flush white, and clean) the relation
between clarity and transparency, the relation between
the reprogramming of the domestic interior and the
burdensome pain of reformatting behaviors to fall in
line with the expectations of the ideals of pure living
the relation between sexual contact and spatial awareness
the relation between the master bedroom and the children's
rooms, with an at least conventional degree of privacy
rendering the erotic translucent as it is contained, the
relation between the voyeuristic pleasures of picture
windows and the guilt that shirks judgment, the relation
between the meal and the mirror, the relation between
a veritable army of new practitioners and their hungry prey
the relation between her hand on the glass curtain and his
pipe curled around the soft plastic edge of his ashtray
the relation between the psychosexual resolution offered by
domestic realms and the anarchic drippiness of the woods
the relation between cultural demands and social realities
the relation between organic life and the phenomena of products

the continuity between material and psychic energy, the relation
between the frigidity of neurosis and the mystic freedom of
energetic redistribution, the relation between making it rain
and curing cancer, the relations among climate control, better
sex, improved health, and happiness itself, the stubby concern
dispelling itself and wiggling over the model of comprehensive
satisfaction, the relation between I and someone else, intercourse
with purveyors, the relation between the obscenity of nature and
the vapidity of an architectural prophylactic, the relation between
needs and desires, the fundamental argument of a semiotics
of the unconscious, the fluid merging of the outside and inside
the relation between what you get and the mad advocate's long
negotiation, the relation between history and his new intimacy
the relation between the picture of pleasure and the emotional
desert of modern life, the relation between a refrigerator and a
throbbing psychosomatic phenomenon, the ways the walls and
planes dynamically slip and slide, the relation between dogma
and its energy source, the proliferation of reflective surfaces
the inside is thrown into the distance, comfortable and glowing
the relation between what we see before us and life-supporting
life-protecting parcels of a wider setting, the essential question.

I Miss the 90s

"You have to accept it!" pearling abuse,
the kids chased through the cannery
and champions followed; the bully lost,
they hid in a storm drain (remembering
how to cruise). Celebration is the wrong word.
"You did then what the dark erases,"
primitive pleasure and civilized pain,
everything on sale, blurred into the trees.
An alien violence ravaged the territory
spreading from opportunity to malice:
"I will never resign, I will never surrender."
The virus needs it to survive but, in living,
kills the host. At least there were those
halcyon days of tobacco and mercenary
endowment, when a total voice portended,
"I miss the 90s, I miss feeling in place."
Sweet bruises mar skin, oceans of absolutes
just brutalizing with a chair leg (wham,
wham, wham!) the soft and hallowed fabric
of compliance, of a chorus line of sick men,
"We find the defendant to be guilty as charged."
It doesn't matter, it didn't before; all that
hangs in the balance is already gone. There is
an argument for forgetting to be born, gunshots
and gravy spilling into the opponents' mouths,
"We can't both be right!" strung out in absentia.

Find now where the treasure quells, there's a pale
young imp slithering down the nervous system,
paralyzing faith to the excuse of a waltz.
The drama of small things takes up so much time.

For Light

I want to be a child again because
Of the architecture of cloudlessness
And diffraction by apertures that draw
Structural lightness thinly across this
Gray ceiling that I thought a firmament
Of such ecstatic possibilities
When both of us together looked at it
And understood incomprehensibly
But then distances dulled our able will
We stumble forth divorced of perception
And dream we are illuminated still
But wake to our present resignation
And since never again we twain shall meet
I must become a child or take defeat.

I Found You There

I.

The door opened. The rug was there. I picked up the rug. I found you there. The door was locked. I picked up the rug. You opened the door. I put down the rug. The door was gone. I found you there. I picked up the rug. The door was there. I walked through the door. The rug was there. I picked up the rug. And you weren't there. I put down the rug. You saw me there. The door was gone. The rug was there. The door was there. You stepped on the rug. I saw you there. I stepped on the rug. The rug was gone. I found you there. The door opened. The rug was there. I picked up the rug. The door was locked. I found you there. The door wasn't locked. The door was there. I found the rug. The door was closed. I lost the rug. The rug was there. The door opened. I picked up the rug. The door hadn't opened. I found you there. The door was locked. I picked up the rock. My car was blocked. I found you there.

II.

I'm not going to learn to remember to be calm, or loyal, or attractive, and then there's the carpet I can't walk on, might say I'm tired, or I'm sorry, or both. I found you there underneath the tree and you whispered, something seductive, but I forgot it, and I'm falling, or something even more poetic. I'm never going to retain all the information that I need to just to see you because I'm never really sober; I'm just listening. I found you there, out on the lawn, and you held me, chastised my grammar, then forgot me, walked away. I'm not going to live the way I like, the way I used to, because it's painful, I mean expensive, and I'm running out of money. I found you there, in your old car, and I held you, and I told you about my laughter, but you weren't listening, then you lied. I'm not going to fall into this moment of resentment, I should be feeling rather

wicked for all the pain that I've caused others. I found you there inside my bedroom, reading the paper, crying buckets, and I told you I need to leave you, and so then you disappeared. I'm not going to commit another sin of disappointment, but my errors are all glaring, and you're packing up and leaving, and my love forgot my name. I found you there in my arms and you were feeling melancholy, and I said that you looked pretty, and you punched me in the face. I'm not going to forgive you for what you're doing, I mean I think I've been understanding, but this time it's really out of line.

III.

I found you there in the car. I found you there in my bed. I found you there in the car. I found you there. I found you there in the car. I found you there on the rug. I found you there in my arms. I found you there in the car. I found you there. I found you there at the door. I found you there at the mall. I found you there at the car. I found you there. I found you there in the car. I found you there at the door. I found you there. I found you there. I found you there in the car. I found you there in the dark. I found you there in my arms. I found you there. I found you there. I found you there asleep. I found you there in the car. I found you there in my bed. I found you there in my bed. I found you there in the car. I found you there in my bed. I found you there. I found you there on the road. I found you there on the roof. I found you there. I found you there at the door. I found you there at the car. I found you there in the tree. I found you there in the tree. I found you there on the rug. I found you there in the car. I found you there. I found you there. I found you there. I found you there in the shower. I found you there on the rug. I found you there. I found you there in the car. I found you there in the car. I found you there in the rain. I found you there in my arms. I found you there in my bed. I found you there. I found you there on the rug. I found you there. I found you there at the door. I found you there at the door. I found you there on the roof. I found you there at the door. I found you there in the car. I found

you there in the shower. I found you there at the mall. I found you
there. I found you there. I found you there in the dark. I found you
there in my arms. I found you there in my arms. I found you there
at the car. I found you there in the car. I found you there in the car.
I found you there in my arms. I found you there in my bed. I found
you there. I found you there. I found you there in the tree. I found
you there. I found you there in the tree. I found you there. I found
you there in the tree. I found you there in the dark. I found you
there. I found you there in the car. I found you there at the car. I
found you there at the mall. I found you there. I found you there.
I found you there in my arms. I found you there on the rug. I found
you there in my bed. I found you there. I found you there on the
road. I found you there asleep. I found you there. I found you there.
I found you there. I found you there. I found you there at the door.
I found you there at the car. I found you there at the car. I found
you there on the rug. I found you there in the car. I found you there.
I found you there in my arms. I found you there in the dark. I found
you there in the tree. I found you there. I found you there in the
tree. I found you there. I found you there. I found you there in the
rain. I found you there in the tree. I found you there at the car. I
found you there in my bed. I found you there at the car. I found
you there at the mall. I found you there. I found you there on the
rug. I found you there. I found you there. I found you there on the
road. I found you there in my bed. I found you there at the mall. I
found you there in the dark. I found you there in my arms. I found
you there. I found you there in the car. I found you there. I found
you there. I found you there. I found you there. I found you there.
I found you there. I found you there. I found you there. I found you
there. I found you there. I found you there. I found you there. I
found you there. I found you there. I found you there. I found you
there. I found you there. I found you there. I found you there. I
found you there. I found you there. I found you there. I found you
there. I found you there. I found you there. I found you there. I
found you there in my arms. I found you there in the car. I found
you there. I found you there. I found you there. I found you there.
I found you there. I found you there. I found you there. I found you

there. I found you there. I found you there. I found you there. I found you there. I found you there in the car. I found you there at the car. I found you there in my arms. I found you there in the car. I found you there.

IV.

You're done. I found you there. I found you there in love. The mattress is on the floor with my stomach. I used to care. I found you there. You're done. Making homes. I found you there. I found you there caring. I'm fun. I'm picking up the telephone. You're alone. You're done. I found you there alone. You're done. I passed out on the rug. I found you there in denial. Every time you're done. We're driving away. I found you there. My life is a widening cloud. I found you there on the train. You're done. We shop weekends at the mall. I found you there. I opened the door for the rug salesman. You're done. We're together. I found you there. It was around the time the world stopped making sense. The sky is fine. I found you there. I found you there with gentle kisses. You're done. I'm waiting for my money. You bought a one-way ticket to the West Coast. I found you there on the West Coast. You're done. We lost ourselves in the parking lot. I found you there. We had a fight. I found you there. I asked you if you were sure. The window was never replaced. You're done. We were wet in the rain. I found you there on the bridge. I crawled through constant pressure. The medication ran out and we almost died. You're done. We sold the car to buy jewelry. I found you there. I found you there in my arms. I placed an ad in the newspaper. I have to get to San Francisco. You're done. I have to get to the beguine. I found you there buying gifts. My despair is like a rug rolled up. I found you there in Los Angeles. I found you there. You're done. In my arms you didn't do well. The train just crashed or something. I found you there. I closed the door upon you. The West Coast is on the floor with the rug. You're done. Making homes. We never moved fast. I wrote you a letter and burned it. I found you there on the couch. We drank wine from the Mission

San Diego de Alcalá. We are all gone. You're done. I'm picking up a shard of the broken window. I mean my heart. I found you there in the magazine. I'm wrapped up in the rug. I found you there. I'm done. I found you there. You're done. I found you there. I found you there. You're done.

V.

I found you there in situations. I found you there in love. I found you there finally. I found you there in love. I found you there in good health. I found you there in situations. I found you there in love. I found you there at the mall. I found you there in the city. I found you there in good health. I found you there in the city. I found you there in love. I found you there in my arms. I found you there buying gifts. I found you there in situations. I found you there at the park. I found you there building. I found you there in good health. I found you there in my arms. I found you there at the mall. I found you there on the horse. I found you there at sea. I found you there in the chair. I found you there in love. I found you there in bad health. I found you there with the jar. I found you there in the tree. I found you there with the book. I found you there in love. I found you there at the mall. I found you there on the planet. I found you there in good health. I found you there in what. I found you there in no. I found you there at the mall. I found you there in my arms. I found you there at the car. I found you there at school. I found you there at the writing desk. I found you there at sea. I found you there in good health. I found you there at sea. I found you there in the clouds. I found you there on the train. I found you there in love. I found you there in good health. I found you there at the park. I found you there at the bar. I found you there with the book. I found you there on the land. I found you there on the horse. I found you there in my arms. I found you there in love. I found you there with numbers. I found you there at the mall. I found you there in the tree. I found you there at the car. I found you there in love. I found you there on the rug. I found you there with numbers.

I found you there at the door. I found you there in love. I found you there at the mall. I found you there in my arms. I found you there with the rock. I found you there buying gifts. I found you there in situations. I found you there with the lesson. I found you there in the clouds. I found you there building. I found you there in love. I found you there in the building. I found you there in my arms. I found you there in love. I found you there in the car. I found you there with the book. I found you there at the mall. I found you there in good health. I found you there on the planet. I found you there in love. I found you there in what. I found you there in my arms. I found you there at the mall. I found you there in love. I found you there in no. I found you there in the tree. I found you there in situations. I found you there eventually. I found you there in bad health. I found you there with the jar. I found you there on the rug. I found you there at the bar. I found you there building. I found you there in the building. I found you there in love. I found you there in my arms. I found you there at sea. I found you there with the jar. I found you there at the mall. I found you there in the chair. I found you there building. I found you there in love. I found you there in my arms. I found you there in love. I found you there in my arms. I found you there in love. I found you there in the chair. I found you there in my arms. I found you there in love. I found you there in my arms. I found you there in love. I found you there in my arms. I found you there in love. I found you there in my arms. I found you there in love. I found you there in my arms. I found you there in love. I found you there in my arms. I found you there in love. I found you there with numbers. I found you there. I found you there in my arms. I found you there in love. I found you there in my arms. I found you there in love. I found you there in my arms. I found you there in love. I found you there in my arms. I found you there in love. I found you there in my arms. I found you there in my arms. I found you there in my arms. I found you there in love. I found you there in love. I found you there in my arms. I found you there in love. I found you there. I found you there. I found you there. I found you there. I found you there. I found you there. I found you there. I found you there. I found you there. I found you there. I found you there. I found you there. I found you there. I

found you there. I found you there. I found you there. I found you there. I found you there. I found you there. I found you there. I found you there. I found you there in my arms. I found you there in love.

VI.

I found you there in situations. I mean I found you there on the rug. I mean this is our planet and this is our life and this is my house and I found you there. I found you there giving me that look. I mean I found you there at the door. I mean the mattress is on the floor with my stomach and I found you there. I found you there in my arms. I mean I found you there driving toward the West Coast. I mean you robbed the bank stole the car and are on the run from the law and I found you there. I found you there punishing. I mean I found you there smashing the mirror. I mean I rolled up the rug and said give me my stuff and you gave me that look and I found you there. I found you there at the mall. I mean I found you there locking the door. I mean the sales are unbelievable so let's get in the car and go to the mall and I found you there. I found you there in my bed. I mean I found you there picking up the rock. I mean I went to the kitchen and I pulled up all the tiles and I looked down under there and I found you there. I found you there in love. I mean I found you there in the car. I mean I can't remember my name and looked up at the clouds and I found you there. I found you there in the dark. I mean I found you there closing up. I mean the end is near and the planet is cold and the law is being lawless and the sky is gray and the ground is quaking and the cars won't start and the shop windows are broken and my heart is broken and my fate is foretold and the mall is closed forever and I looked at what was in my arms and I found you there. I found you there. I found you there.

VII.

I found you there. I found you there. I found you there finally. I found you there in church. I found you there finally. I found you there. I found you there in my arms. I found you there with numbers. I found you there. I found you there at the mall. I found you there. I found you there at the mall. I found you there in my arms. I found you there in my arms. I found you there at church. I found you there telling. I found you there in love. I found you there in love. I found you there in the car. I found you there in love. I found you there in love. I found you there finally. I found you there in love. I found you there at the mall. I found you there. I found you there learning. I found you there at the door. I found you there in church. I found you there. I found you there learning. I found you there in the dark. I found you there. I found you there. I found you there in my arms. I found you there. I found you there building. I found you there finally. I found you there in my arms. I found you there at the car. I found you there in my arms. I found you there at the car. I found you there in my arms. I found you there. I found you there. I found you there building. I found you there in situations. I found you there. I found you there building. I found you there in church. I found you there in my arms. I found you there at the door. I found you there with numbers. I found you there finally. I found you there in my arms. I found you there. I found you there at the car. I found you there at the car. I found you there on the rug. I found you there building. I found you there in the dark. I found you there at the car. I found you there in the car. I found you there telling. I found you there. I found you there in church. I found you there in situations. I found you there on the rug. I found you there on the rug. I found you there at the mall. I found you there. I found you there on the rug. I found you there at the mall. I found you there in love. I found you there in my arms. I found you there. I found you there at the door. I found you there. I found you there in the rain. I found you there in my arms. I found you there in my arms. I found you there at the mall. I found you there

learning. I found you there. I found you there learning. I found you there in situations. I found you there learning. I found you there in my arms. I found you there at the mall. I found you there at the mall. I found you there in my arms. I found you there at the mall. I found you there in my arms. I found you there at the mall. I found you there in my arms. I found you there at the mall. I found you there in the dark. I found you there at the mall. I found you there in my arms. I found you there at the mall. I found you there in situations. I found you there learning. I found you there in the rain. I found you there. I found you there in the rain. I found you there. I found you there. I found you there at the car. I found you there on the rug. I found you there at the car. I found you there in the car. I found you there on the rug. I found you there at church. I found you there in my arms. I found you there learning. I found you there in the dark. I found you there telling. I found you there. I found you there finally. I found you there telling. I found you there in the rain. I found you there finally. I found you there learning. I found you there. I found you there in the rain. I found you there on the rug. I found you there. I found you there in love. I found you there. I found you there. I found you there at church. I found you there telling. I found you there at church. I found you there caring. I found you there. I found you there caring. I found you there in my arms. I found you there in love. I found you there in love. I found you there finally. I found you there with numbers. I found you there learning. I found you there with numbers. I found you there learning. I found you there with numbers. I found you there. I found you there learning. I found you there in the rain. I found you there in love. I found you there at the door. I found you there at the mall. I found you there with numbers. I found you there in church. I found you there. I found you there in my arms. I found you there in my arms. I found you there in the dark. I found you there telling. I found you there at the car. I found you there learning. I found you there on the rug. I found you there on the rug. I found you there building. I found you there on the rug. I found you there. I found you there on the rug. I found you there in my arms. I found you there. I found you there telling. I found you there in love. I

found you there in the dark. I found you there caring. I found you there at the car. I found you there in situations. I found you there. I found you there in love. I found you there in the car. I found you there in the dark. I found you there in my arms. I found you there in the car. I found you there finally. I found you there telling. I found you there in the car. I found you there with numbers. I found you there at the door. I found you there learning. I found you there at the mall. I found you there learning. I found you there at church. I found you there at church. I found you there in my arms. I found you there learning. I found you there at church. I found you there in the dark. I found you there in my arms. I found you there with numbers. I found you there in love. I found you there at the car. I found you there in the car. I found you there in love. I found you there caring. I found you there at the door. I found you there in the rain. I found you there in the car. I found you there. I found you there in my arms. I found you there. I found you there in my arms. I found you there finally. I found you there in the alphabet. I found you there. I found you there in the dictionary. I found you there. I found you there in the alphabet. I found you there in love. I found you there in love. I found you there in the dictionary. I found you there in love. I found you there in the dictionary. I found you there in the alphabet. I found you there in love. I found you there. I found you there in love. I found you there in the alphabet. I found you there. I found you there in the alphabet. I found you there in love. I found you there in the alphabet. I found you there. I found you there in the dictionary. I found you there in the alphabet. I found you there. I found you there in love. I found you there in the dictionary. I found you there in the alphabet. I found you there in love. I found you there in the dictionary. I found you there in the dictionary. I found you there in the alphabet. I found you there in love. I found you there in the alphabet. I found you there in love. I found you there in the alphabet. I found you there. I found you there in the alphabet. I found you there in love. I found you there in the alphabet. I found you there. I found you there in the dictionary. I found you there. I found you there in love. I found you there. I found you there in the dictionary. I found you there in love. I found

you there on the mountain. I found you there. I found you there in love. I found you there. I found you there in love. I found you there in the alphabet. I found you there in love. I found you there. I found you there. I found you there in love. I found you there. I found you there in love. I found you there. I found you there in love. I found you there. I found you there in the alphabet. I found you there in love. I found you there in love. I found you there finally. I found you there.

Drowning in Fun

Rude descent via escalator:
Auspicious compassion,
Some hired gun dashed in!
If he goes, she knows he'll take her.

Hungover and licking my wounds,
Could we be more dishonest?
The foundation was flawless,
And misery's always in bloom.

I'll learn to love my abusers
The day that the world grows sage.
Till then: my magnificent rage,
Piss, and nail polish remover.

Amuck, those postmodern monsters
(Being a poet is so hard;
Not a real job, like a lifeguard);
We've run out of planets to conquer!

Entrusting herself to a dark ride:
Somehow she will manage
The mirth of brain damage,
Her problems wiped out in a landslide.

No way to know the evil done,
An ecology of wreck
Drooling down a burdened neck.
We're already drowning in fun.

How Do You Know This Is For Real?

this bridge is fully dangerous
strung frowned over a question
or whatever the landscape was
forget about it or take a drink
you need a sensitive fella who
might guide your line as your
trying falls into the hurt about
the knife of remembrance the
rad area where consequences
inflate into drastic dreams for
a couple poets holding hands
at the political sunset of truth
        How do you know this is for real
the final plane lands crashing
in that river twixt the banks of
whatever the memory of which
stimulates you embarrassingly
before the water flows: computer
after everything's done: computer
smile away thoughts of the boy
who brought you to your senses
disasters or accidents are hungry
fair warning never comes family
means next to nothing meaning
means less than family bridges
are franchises for the need you

feel when all the lights go out
any motive remains unclear

How do you know this is for real
mere poetry doesn't do it still
the proletariat earns and fucks
in what they can afford while
the luxury of careless audacity
turns this population on tonight
when what goes for most folks
drunk drives into a storefront
most poets know how to drive
forever is not sophisticated or
existence is what philosophers
party for waiting for the inquiry

How do you know this is for real
what a fab old bash laughs death
the legendary evil hath returned
so mundane it doesn't even hurt
costumed jolly within that lurks
the last question one ever hears

How do you know this is for real
the glimmer of the really scary
not of the "god is dead" variety
but an assaultive nation turning
around like a tanker in the night
machines more drunk with fright
than a soldier finding a spider
in his upturned helmet praying

to the sun the kind of achy riddle
posed to teenagers and presidents
as a way to reconcile the century
and bury the bones of command
      How do you know this is for real
      How do you know this is for real?
ask from the bridge edge and jump

Mrs. Whitman

there was I pity my son a time
of so much practice and
a quiet trembling fascination
and when a man came forth
under the residual
and his name was death

an abacus rose
alarming and full of leisurely deer
shining tenses everywhere
giving out bones
I don't think after you
being amongst them

remembering friends I saw
each experience and examples
of woman I saw that each
in amazement and anger
their mouth is a hell mouth
their mouth is an hour

now what my mother told me
of when she saw nearly grown
an Indigenous woman came betide
her at the breakfast table

profuse and half enveloped
tall borne for all pliant limbs

the genders askance
creepily dithering over our
supper of mornings
damages in the rough
shade well and bode
and speak as I spoke

I thought of everything
sometimes we are sorry
but it seems a forthright
you know by the writing
it must amaze in difference
I make a few lines as to begin

skin has a mimetic power
what a stupid man
and the balance
this insolvent house
means nothing to the
courage of my love

amidst the humanity
nobody has seen this before
I bellflower.

The Great Bird Will Take the Universe

I.

When researches, normally
                  blacken the sublime
ascribe material for these reasons
objects that concern   everything
recognized—unpublished development in him:
        severe in the end, according to the words
        his failure art.
What prevented the cause?
Remarkable architect
unusual refinement. It is indeed quite possible
activity, security, form of research
dead bodies and human beings—flying machines.
        Distorted vestiges, experimental attempts:
his works excuses
then days would pass.
The evidence is seen to be a symptom. Technical
miscarriage
which he left unfinished,   building
contradictions. A certain everyone   at a time.
        Pleasure described this feminine
        deprive animals. Study good and
evil. Biographical hero's mental
following sentence.   Pretty writing

posthumous problems.   A struggle

artist   surprise everything sexual.

      Womb

never embraced a woman in passion—

       as a model he surrounded

        his death was named without sharing.

Existence did not extend to sexual activity.

       There is way emotional

       scientific problem

       the way writers in plastic terms.

His confession has no right to love

—and the same is repeated:

love springs from the object.

You will be able to love it   only

the process   only.

      (Not proper love.)

Time understands that it happens

everyone, hatred as he does

it really seems to have been so.

      Research did not love

      about the significance

        he was indifferent.

Negative signs transformed into intellectual reality

lack divine is behind activity

climax when knowledge won

emotion praised language.

      A development, mode

example teaches   stormy consumes
      beyond love instead of loving.
There are some further consequences.

II.

Laws of light, colors, shadows and
perspective, the imitation of nature
the same value branches the subject
the proportions of the human body
vital functions become overwhelming
science was always something kept
away from him. Attempt to exercise
when there was little room.

He saw countless problems arising to see the work of art.
Most exhausting explanation: in the subject's early child
hood we make the place for example—instead of loving
we venture. There has been a sexual special intensity.
The curiosity of small children questions an end because
researches are directed to the question.
Information, meaning serious adults—
                    inside the mother's body.

The period of infantile sexual
repression opens the whole of
the subject. Play by education
in this way gives an effective

impetus—the outbreak of a
    neurotic illness.

Color becomes
a solution.
Most perfect
unconscious desire—
research becomes
sexual activity.
Complete processes
are absent
—there operate
sexual themes.
Research homosexuality.

    The secret
    would appear
    a model
    in service
    of research.
    Some picture
    in years
    seems foolish
    for material
    when information
    escapes attention.

About youth we know very little.

A grave father in those days
fathers his mother probably
a girl married the only piece
of information comes from a
document of the household
of the marriage remained
childless   little town
up in his father's house he
did not leave the house the
year name was already. That

                    is all.

        There is only one place.

Information about vultures suddenly interrupts
                    memory. Very early sprung was
always vultures earliest memories was in my
vultures and opened my mouth many times
against my lips.
What have memory that a person should memory
period is not impossible. Any means this   memory
namely that a vulture opened the child's mouth
with an end to fabulous difficulties. Our judgment
vultures memory. The vulture formed a date in
which memories originate. The moment of being
experienced and afterward repeated is already past
in the process of writing history.

        It was an age of historical writing
        not historians.

III.

History of the past rather than
the past—wrong interpretation orders
motives for writing history,   mirroring
memories of his story about the vulture.
            Only time might be satisfied—
this story   to reject the body
        all the distortions and misunderstandings
the past, they are what forms
experience. In disclosing the historical
legendary material, he remembers childhood indifference.
            He himself does not understand
                            priceless pieces
the techniques of excellent light, concealed
so that many other studies have met no
better fate.   The eyes of the vulture
seem to recall examples from special language.
Familiar symbols in other languages—the situation
of a vulture beating vigorously the idea. A sexual
act   in which the penis
                    is put into the mouth.
Fantasy found women, passive homosexuals
who play the woman in. The reader will
                            restrain
allow memory the very first time—
significance, in the most unambiguous fashion:
meaning, a dream, a vision, or delirium.

Analysis has not yet spoken   its last   word.

Sculptures, being in love, are found by doctors.

Difficulty informs satisfaction—
                         the most innocent kind only repeats.
    The most innocent kind only repeats.
Comfortable into our mouth and sucked at it
a penis resembles the stage and the shape, position
under the belly. Pleasure remains a familiar function.
Now we understand the memory of experience.
The vulture period is merely his mother
human beauty transformed into a passive homosexual
being the question of homosexuality
                         homosexual fact
—his mother, we find, his mother   the vulture
does it happen to be found?
Childhood is to separate memory
his mother the vulture was aware of his father his mother.
The fact of birth is in his vulture—himself, a vulture child
when that happened it is here. Mother with his poor absence
his father married a lady of good birth this marriage his
house. Disappointment had probably grown up an attractive
young boy.   The vulture of life
has elapsed of his mother
before he could then it was too late.
The outside established memories are built on
                         elements in his fact vulture

alone with his mother, was that the child

his early problem began with special sexual researches

—his curiosity, the vulture.

The vulture of his memory

the context, a bright light

against a homosexual situation.

The mother has been turned into a   vulture

in which language substitutes the   vulture

anything signifies a penis—understand activity.

The bird is a mother with a mark of masculinity

                     in view of this

                     absurdity we are

                     at a loss how to

reduce this to any

meaning.

We should despair

                  we reflect the past   we have

given up meaning.

Is there any reason why a memory

should give us an explanation?

The fact is intended to embody the mother

which is the opposite of everything.

Sexual theories: when the mother

is dominated his body exists, all human beings

destroyed perception, he cannot find

a penis in girls, little girls had a penis but

it was cut off and in its place

was left a wound.

So dear under the influence of this threat

a new light will tremble for masculinity

despite unhappy creatures.

The cruel punishment has already fallen

complex women value intense desire

genitals culminate her.

The discovery of disgust becomes

        fetishistic reverence

            —puberty

leaves indelible traces

from primitive time.

Time suffers in the process.

Something more contained changed

the mother is a situation

when we remember the historical homosexual

(having behaved as emotionally homosexual)

the question is forced upon existence

          —his mother is homosexuality.

We know the homosexual does exist

and in fact,   homosexual men

impose representing themselves.

Theoretically, being is a stage, a third sex:

they are,   they claim.

Men find pleasure in men and have been

in women.

Homosexuality offers homosexuals

but all so far have yielded
the same male homosexual subjects
a rule their mother.
Our intense childhood is afterward forgotten
the father I have occasionally seen
the son made the correct object.
A transformation mechanism we do not yet understand
succumbs to mother
he puts place with her
his model in the new objects.
Love
grows up. Childhood
love finds the object.   Love—narcissism.
Reflection of everything changed the lovely name.
A man who becomes homosexual remains
in this way fixated on image.   His love
to pursue boys, the male object,   repeats
over.   His mother: the mechanism
(by which he acquired his homosexuality).

Homosexuality is quite obvious
homosexuals are not comprehensive
reasons called homosexuality may arise.

Processes process, but we know not what they are—
the particular process is homosexuality:
        we require what we cannot reject.

Our homosexual is unknown
homosexuality not usually traced
we should not have any cause for entering
 the form of homosexuality.

The problem possible
we require a strong vulture.

IV.

We find anything untransformed
the homosexual, emphasized, allowed
                    to be reckoned.
           He treated them with kindness and
           consideration, nursed them as a mother
           nurses her children—a mother chosen
           for her beauty.
Not for none of them
after his death they disappeared
history works like the diary of other mortals.
           Complete silence, quoted by biographers
                    no record or any other evidence.
Bad habits
a pair of trousers and a jacket
my purse was never possible.
           Small weaknesses   behind vivid light
The death of the mother was
his mother. Process processes insignificant intensity

his act is performed in his mother's funeral.

   He was to her erotically

     the subsequent love did not allow

     knowledge as something intelligible.

We have learnt the funeral.

        Manner that his mother

        betrayed erotic life.

His own objects dominated us.

Homosexuality succeeded in the emergence of

       the situation.

Meaning was exactly that type.

    I became a homosexual.

We have not done with vulture

in words, many times against my lips.

Mother linking his mother the

vulture activity. The mouth zone—

a second memory.

This may be translated: my mother

is compounded—the memory

   of being and being his mother.

Nature has the artist from himself

(means he creates strangers)

emotion is nothing   witness memory

childhood something

impression before a work of art

   demonstration within anyone.

Female subjects produce the most   interpretation

erotic women between and between men

—ruthlessly demanding men as if they were alien beings.

He employed artifices.

We fancy lady taken:

the delicate details achieve the person

let us leave her smile

we cannot assume her face

      not herself, the conclusion

this model spells   this situation

         beheld   at last.

Something in him had an old memory

memory had never aroused his childhood

      his dreams literarily formed the subject.

        It is not intended to prove anything—

      some heads of laughing women

      some children's heads were beautiful.

We learn a career of objects

we have   the vulture.

Reproductions of his repetitions

begin to smile.   His mother

had lost it when he found it again

      found it again in the lady.

V.

Child is not possible
composition—
in his mind the
memory of his   mother.
We may permit
less beautiful
treatment of
subjects. The   woman
plays unmistakably.
Mysterious quiet: known
versions. Perhaps
time draws   vulture.
In his house
he found details.
His mother was
these circumstances.

Childhood watched over
          mother
who must have portrayed a young woman
—beauty has given the boy two mothers.
Smile the motherhood the same way
          he had two mothers
he was between and tender. His mother was
his wife.   The design shapes him
earlier, she was

87

she was forced to give

up her son, the

unfortunate woman.

She had once given up a confirmation.

We find grown

the memory of his   mother

would to search and   suffer.

     Mother's privations were

the violence.

     He remained his vulture, was

only too natural.

Her memories forced her father to fondle

him.   Husband him of

his masculinity. She enjoyed no husband

like all unsatisfied mothers.

     She cares for something

          love represents

     satisfying impulses. Human happiness

must be called perverse.

VI.

Aware the baby marriage

son becomes the rival

rapture played his mother

forbade desire from lips

reproduce his giving

fact into secret dares

penetrate the vulture.
Love denied unhappiness
representing his mother
—mother triumphed.
The boy in his female natures.

Error, the father
death of the sentence
time—repetition
already written
(at the beginning).
Nothing processes
he learnt ago
forgetting repetition
significant repetition—
an excellent means
of affective color.
My poor father
displacement died
all emotions.
A position—
his wives died
he married
his two daughters.
Father plays
psychosexual place
escape identity
gain house

his mother found
homosexuality
about puberty.
Sexual significance
kept erotic servants
responsibility for nothing
almost nothing
a copy—his father
his father, a gentleman
therefore never
never ceased to play
(to show what his
father really looks like).

A father created about them
father's concern
news died in a dungeon
someone of his father
the fact he was
in what he said.

Father damage against father
becomes the first modern
scientist. The man since
time. Teaching constantly
repeating. Man had already
forced the little boy.
We translate the mother

in most other human beings.
The existence of sexual father
by his father when everyone has
found unable to escape
father complex in father
parental complex. Biologically
speaking, father breaks down.
Child's ideas of them dates
childhood in attempts to deny
(illness is easily explained).

Astray, he calculated in hesitation
the last church made human
show lack for ultimate cause.
All these noble secrets:
human beings, subjects removed
from the world. Childhood
problems of sexuality
research transparent—problem
of birds, special attention.

The great bird will take the universe.

The art of himself—
he probably hoped we know
from dreams what bliss
is expected.
Why do so many people dream?

A bird is only a disguise for words:
a bridge—we recognize children
as a large bird. We find the phallus
as having wings.
The male organ is called
the bird.
All these are fragments
from which we learn nothing.

VII.

An adult happy time   children
        but if children themselves—
future, without any information.
        Grown-up games—
aviation has infantile erotic
        form a special problem
the violent disguise of childhood.

        Maturity in mechanical sex
        —slight changes in meaning
        the same subject.
        Frustrated toys: he got
        a soft lump.
        He filled with air
        he made wings.
        He put it in a box and terrified
        friends carefully

forced people to become transparent

gradually became transparent and filled with air.

The room is illustrated by genius

the same playful form

devoid of example. Manuscripts

conclude while he was there.

Play vanished from his childhood if in his childhood

the highest erotic bliss

is never again attained.

Blind the fact

all pathology

clothe things in him

—pretext and disguise

pathology does not, no one

should be blamed   never promised.

We discover special reasons: emotional

traces (smooth), life's struggles

human weakness, strange fact

regrettable fantasies, fascinating

secrets—penetrating his

love, his thirst.

An attempt by learning from him

we make sacrifices from childhood

the awkward phrase never goes

nerve case   the light gained in the field

the tragic mark of failure.

A human being substitute for
the practical concept of illness
place to what are known.

       Summarize the picture
art and science—these statements
provoked mysterious men.
Attraction
instinctual passions
       subdued a manner
(remarkably).

       The truth limits biography
       circumstances support physical mechanisms
the basis for his nature of reactions
       transformations explained: operation
of fate. Blame methods or material.
             The failure
to pronounce
could be dealt with
in no other way.

       The person had to maintain
       the accident.   His birth
       and his mother
       influence this phase   of childhood.
We must recognize
freedom which cannot be resolved.
       Means has no right to claim the consequence.
We are left with special instincts
—instincts in the foundation

of mental character

the function

the tendency

        intimacy we must admit

           the male

we will not remain along that path.

A man renders manifestation

experiences of light

beauty based on a melancholy career

his achievements and misfortunes—

        painted in the childhood fantasy

of vulture.

In fact, everything lacks any connection

with our wishes and illusions.

        Our childhood

is no longer possible.

    The universe forces her way into experience.

Grown Ups

I found you there in my parents' backyard
You were just looking right into the sun
I told you quit acting like some retard
You smiled and said you knew but it was fun
We climbed a tree and there I took your hand
And with a razor blade I carved my name
In the pale flesh covered by your watchband
And then I rubbed your jeans until you came
Presently we reclined in the warm grass
And closed our eyes to look at our red lids
You said something I couldn't hear at last
We were confident and unworried kids
You jumped off the Eiffel Tower the year
I declared loneliness was my career.

Obliquities

"Magic Bridge" is a sestina. "The House of There Is" is an erasure of the sermon "Sinners in the Hands of an Angry God" by Jonathan Edwards. "Nincompoop Insolence Aria" is a translation of the "La donna è mobile" canzone by Francesco Maria Piave from the opera *Rigoletto* by Giuseppe Verdi. "Fag City" is a sonnet. "The Demand for a Sign" is a treatment of Mark 8:11 from the New Testament of the *Holy Bible*. "Thinking of You" repurposes textual fragments from the English language examples in *French Grammar: A Complete Reference Guide* by Daniel J. Calvez. "The Resignation" is the full text of the resignation speech of New York governor Eliot Spitzer; repeating, each time translated into more and different languages and then back to English using the application Babelfish. "Those That Belong to the Emperor" is a sonnet. "Handsome Boy Full of Arrows" is a meditation on the figure of Saint Sebastian at his martyrdom. "For Example" repurposes a textual fragment from *A Course in General Linguistics* by Ferdinand de Saussure. "The Gettysburg Address" is the eponymous speech by president Abraham Lincoln with every word rearranged in alphabetical order. "More Right Now a Piano" is an ekphrastic meditation on Alice Neel's portrait of Andy Warhol. "Domestic Relations" is based upon the essay "Open the Box: Richard Neutra and the Psychology of the Domestic Environment" by Sylvia Lavin. "For Light" is a sonnet. "Mrs. Whitman" is based upon "Confusion of Tongues" by Michael Moon and Eve Kosofsky Sedgwick, a conversation on the letters of Louisa Whitman to her son Walt, found in *Breaking Bounds: Whitman and American Cultural Studies*, with some language borrowed directly from Walt Whitman's poem "The Sleepers." "The Great Bird Will Take the Universe" is an erasure of the essay "Leonardo da Vinci: a Memory of His Childhood" by Sigmund Freud. "Grown Ups" is a sonnet; the use of an ableist slur in this poem does not reflect the views or conversational vocabulary of the author but is intended to characterize the speaker during a period of immature youth.

Acknowledgements

Many of the poems in this volume have previously appeared in the chapbooks *Satan* and *Wow*, *Where Do You Come from*, *Upside-Down Land?*, the anthologies *Future Perfect*, *Into*, *Poems in the Aftermath*, *The Sonnets: Translating & Rewriting Shakespeare*, and *Way of the Word*, and the publications *The Brooklyn Rail*, *Correspondence*, *Elderly*, *The Huffington Post*, and *The Physical Poets Home Library*.

Special thanks to Gregory Afinogenov, Priscilla Becker, Rijard Bergeron, Charles Bernstein, Anselm Berrigan, CAConrad, Ben Fama, Robert Fitterman, Michael Gottlieb, Christian Hawkey, Eddie Hopely, Jen Hyde, Kevin Killian, Gregory Laynor, Rachel Levitsky, Richard Loranger, Robert Yerarchmiel Sniderman, and Christopher Sweeney.

ROOF BOOKS
the best in language since 1976

Recent & Selected Titles
• ECHOLOCATION by Evelyn Reilly, 144 p. $17.95
• HOW TO FLIT by Mark Johnson. 104 p. $16.95
• (((...))) by Maxwell Owen Clark. 136 p. $16.95
• THE RECIPROCAL TRANSLATION PROJECT
by Sun Dong & James Sherry. 208 p $22.95
• DETROIT DETROIT by Anna Vitale. 108 p. $16.95
• GOODNIGHT, MARIE, MAY GODHAVE MERCY ON YOUR SOUL
by Marie Buck. 108 p. $16.95
• BOOK ABT FANTASY by Chris Sylvester. 104 p. $16.95
• NOISE IN THE FACE OF by David Buuck. 104 p. $16.95
• PARSIVAL by Steve McCaffery. 88 p. $15.95
• DEAD LETTER by Jocelyn Saidenberg. 94 p. $15.95
• social patience by David Brazil. 136 p. $15.95
• THE PHOTOGRAPHER by Ariel Goldberg. 84 p. $15.95
• TOP 40 by Brandon Brown. 138 p. $15.95
• THE MEDEAD by Fiona Templeton. 314 p. $19.95
• LYRIC SEXOLOGY VOL. 1 by Trish Salah. 138 p. $15.95
• INSTANT CLASSIC by erica kaufman 90 p. $14.95
• A MAMMAL OF STYLE by Kit Robinson
& Ted Greenwald. 96 p. $14.95
• MOTES by Craig Dworkin. 88 p. $14.95
• BOTH POEMS by Anne Tardos. 112 p. $14.95

Roof Books are published by
Segue Foundation
300 Bowery • New York, NY 10012
For a complete list, please visit **roofbooks.com**

Roof Books are distributed by
SMALL PRESS DISTRIBUTION
1341 Seventh Street • Berkeley, CA. 94710-1403.
spdbooks.org